—THE—
ENNEAGRAM
TYPE 8
journal

A Guide to Inner Work & Self-Discovery
for The Challenger

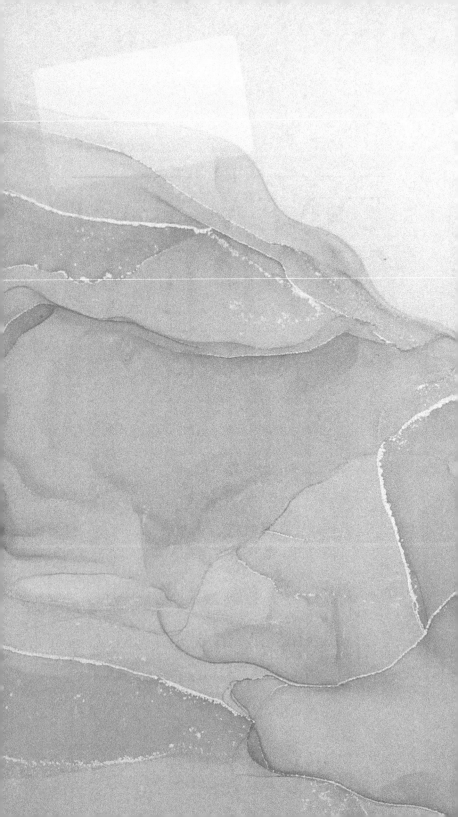

THIS JOURNAL BELONGS TO:

Tradepaper ISBN: 978-1-4019-7908-9
10 9 8 7 6 5 4 3 2 1
1st edition, May 2024

This product uses responsibly sourced papers and/or recycled materials. For more information, see www.hayhouse.com.

Printed and bound by CPI Group (UK) Ltd, Croydon, CR0 4YY

MIX
Paper | Supporting
responsible forestry
FSC® C013604

THE
ENNEAGRAM
TYPE 8
journal

DEBORAH THREADGILL EGERTON, Ph.D.
& LISI MOHANDESSI

HAY HOUSE LLC
Carlsbad, California • New York City
London • Sydney • New Delhi

This journal is dedicated to the
Divine feminine energy
of the women who have
been guiding stars.
Your presence in my life
is the actualization of our
collective dreams come true.

You are gifted with a body that allows you to be here in the present moment, a mind that opens access to unlimited possibilities to be explored, and a heart that holds the enormous capacity to love and be loved.

This is the authentic you. You will find yourself when you accept the beauty of your true nature.

Gratitude for who you are is the first step.

Grace will follow.

Caritas,
Deborah & Lisi

CONTENTS

Introduction 1

The Enneagram 5

Enneagram Type Eight 12

Reflections on Being an Enneagram Eight 22

Reflections on My Early Messages and Experiences 34

Reflections on My Purpose and My "Puzzle Piece" 44

Reflections on How My Eight Energy Shows Up 58

Reflections on Power, Control, and Vulnerability 74

Reflections on My Relationship to Anger 88

Reflections on My Virtue of Innocence 100

Discovering Connections to Other Enneagram Energies 112

Resources for Continued Exploration 130

About the Author 131

*Enjoy your journey, and
may you find love and
light within yourself.*

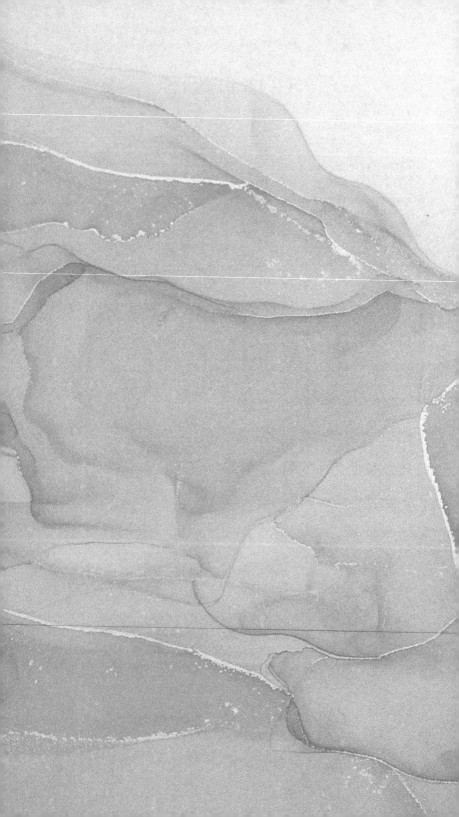

INTRODUCTION

Many of us journey through life pondering the reasons behind our actions and how we can enrich our lives. We seek not only improvement but also a sense of tranquility, productivity, and purpose. Conversations with friends, colleagues, mentors, and partners often echo the advice to "do the work." This phrase never fails to elicit a knowing smile because if it were that simple, we would already be immersed in the process of "doing the work." Yet we continually find ourselves returning to the fundamental question: What is the work?

A deep understanding of oneself is necessary to live a life brimming with abundance, creativity, joy, and love. Self-awareness is a journey inward, a voyage to explore how we present ourselves to the world, and the Enneagram will serve as our guide. Clues about our true selves are sometimes scattered before us, but we often choose to look away from anything that challenges our self-image. This is why the voyage inward, toward self-realization, becomes indispensable in uncovering our genuine, authentic selves.

This journal is thoughtfully crafted to accompany you on this very journey as you harness the insights of the Enneagram. Within these pages you'll encounter an array of writing prompts, mindfulness exercises, inspirational quotes, and grounding meditations for introspection. Each page is a deliberate step along your unique path. It's crucial to remember that this process cannot be hurried or coerced. Guidance on this voyage comes from a source known by many names—God, the Universe, the Divine, Spirit, or a name entirely personal to your experience. All these concepts are interconnected. You need not adhere to any dogmatic religious structure; what truly matters is connecting with that part of you that acknowledges a higher force, shaping and influencing your choices and your path forward.

This journal isn't something you casually dip into; rather, it's an invitation to cultivate a consistent habit of exploring its pages, allowing you to fully embrace the practices within. These pages are designed to guide you toward a profound understanding of why you do what you do.

The Enneagram stands out as a radiant gem among the many personality typing systems, and it beckons with a warm, unique approach centered on uncovering motivations rather than mere behaviors. It opens a doorway to explore the why behind our actions, inviting us to discover the roots of our behaviors. As we delve into this exploration, we find newfound flexibility, unlocking exciting possibilities we may have never imagined before.

We encourage you to delve deeper into the understanding of your dominant Enneagram energy, which is akin to picking up a mirror to gaze upon yourself in a way you've never done before. The idea may initially seem a bit intimidating, but the richness of your life is directly linked to the depth you're willing to explore within your soul.

Your life inherently possesses meaning, purpose, and a trajectory leading toward goodness; it's our natural inclination. Sometimes, we find ourselves needing to reconnect with what truly matters. We might start to wonder and feel disoriented when we sense that we've drifted away from our guiding light. But remember, that guidance hasn't abandoned us; it's possible we've simply strayed from it, unable to see what's right in front of us.

As you embark on this journey, we wish you all the goodness and benefits it has to offer. It's not about reaching a final destination but about following your guiding light, aligning yourself with what's genuine, trustworthy, and good in both the world and within yourself. Return to the pages of this journal daily, allowing your journey to inform you and lead you toward truth, joy, love, light, and goodness. All these elements reside within you, and they'll never abandon you. Sources of love and joy perpetually surround us, and by embracing the truth of goodness in the world, you'll radiate with the light found inside yourself.

This journal is designed as your reference guide and exploratory workbook. The following section will gently guide you through the Enneagram system and provide an overview of Type Eight energy. Within these pages, you'll find a wealth of knowledge about the Enneagram; and using this journal is a chance to reignite your inner connection with your Enneagram Eight energy. Prepare yourself, for your mind will be engaged, your heart will be touched, and your body will respond; all of these experiences, both uplifting and challenging, are an integral part of the journey. We hope you continue to revisit these pages as you further your journey deeper into the Enneagram system.

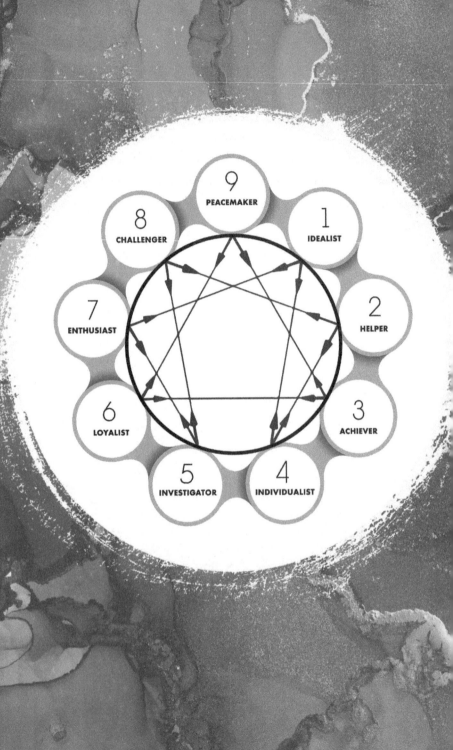

The Enneagram

The Enneagram is an archetypal personality system that combines modern psychological practices with a deep foundation in ancient traditions, religions, cultures, and spiritual practices. It is a model of the human psyche taught as a typology of nine personality archetypes. These types have names that reflect the nine different energies: Eight, Challenger; Nine, Peacemaker; One, Idealist; Two, Helper; Three, Achiever; Four, Individualist; Five, Investigator; Six, Loyalist; and Seven, Enthusiast.

The Enneagram invites you to embark on a journey of self-discovery, unlocking the intricate mechanisms governing your existence. It allows you to delve into the why behind your actions and the how of your daily functioning in pursuit of fulfilling your needs. Unveiling your core motivations, values, fears, and inherent strengths is a perpetual source of insight. Simultaneously, the Enneagram casts light on the egoic patterns that occasionally hinder our progress, thwarting our alignment with our true selves. More significantly, while this insightful system aids us in uncovering our authentic selves, it equally guides us in connecting with others, fostering appreciation, and cultivating genuine presence.

This beginning section is designed to serve as a refresher on the basics of the Enneagram and a quick look into each of the nine types. Remember: the Enneagram is a fluid system that provides access to all nine types, and we encourage you to explore your relationship with all of these energies.

The moment you intentionally chose to use this journal, you began your journey to discover who you really are instead of creating another version of yourself. Or, as people like to say, "the best version of yourself." Your goal now is to find out who you are underneath all the versions of yourself that you have created. Welcome to the journey of your lifetime! May you find joy, peace, acceptance, and belonging in this exploration. May love be your path, and may light shine on every step you take. Most importantly, may you fall deeply in love with the authentic you. The glorious being that you were created to be.

A QUICK OVERVIEW OF THE BASICS OF THE ENNEAGRAM

TYPE/POINT

Each of the nine Enneagram points possesses unique energies and characteristics. When discussing an Enneagram type, we are identifying the specific point on the Enneagram where one embodies the most significant energy. It's important to note that we have access to all nine points on the Enneagram, each contributing to our holistic understanding and personal growth.

CENTERS OF INTELLIGENCE

The Enneagram is explored through three Centers of Intelligence: Body, Heart, and Head. Sometimes, these centers, or triads, are called Body/ Instinctive, Heart/Feeling, and Head/Thinking. Each center has a connection to particular emotions: the Body, anger and rage (Eight, Nine, One); the Heart, shame and guilt (Two, Three, Four); and the Head, fear and anxiety (Five, Six, Seven).

BASIC DESIRE AND BASIC FEAR

We all have inner drive and internalized fear that affect all of our behaviors, beliefs, and actions. You may resonate with all nine basic fears and desires, as we are beings composed of all nine energies; however, you will have the most substantial connection to one corresponding fear and desire of one specific type.

CORE MOTIVATION

The core motivation constantly challenges us to get what we most desire at any given moment while avoiding what we fear that will cause our demise. The core motivation is your internal drive, the reason you wake up in the morning, how you navigate life, and that thing that gets you going or paralyzes you. Think of the core motivation as why you do what you do.

WINGS

The types on either side of your dominant Enneagram energy affect how your type shows up in the world. Every Enneagram type has two wings; however, one of the wings may significantly influence the energy of your dominant Enneagram type.

LINES AND ARROWS

The Enneagram lines and arrows, also referred to as the stress and security points or directions of growth and stress, connect the types across the map. There are multiple ways of using the lines and arrows when we see them as connections to pick up specific qualities at specific times. We can move freely between these connections, picking up positive and negative energies as we need them to create a warning system and a path for growth.

PASSION: THE WAY WE SUFFER — PERSONAL CHALLENGE

The passions represent the nine main ways we lose our center, become more susceptible to personality distortions, and become disoriented from reality. We can refer to each of the passions as the way in which each type suffers.

FIXATION: HOW WE GET STUCK — THE TRAP

We all have a way of becoming trapped in our personality, which we see play out through the fixation. These "traps" are mental blocks we hold on to when attempting to justify our reality.

VIRTUE: OUR TRUE NATURE — THE GIFT

Honoring our true selves and who we become develops when we land in our virtue. These specific characteristics manifest through the emotional awareness of the authentic self, and the letting go of ego, self-deception, and dynamic vices. When we access our virtue, we become selfless and altruistic in our actions, feelings, and beliefs.

INSTINCTS

The Instincts, sometimes referred to as Subtypes and Instinctual Variants, within each Enneagram energy are Self-Preservation, Social, and Sexual (sometimes referred to as One-on-One). The Instincts can be mirrored in the three drives for survival: preserving life and focusing on physical needs, mutual cooperation and creating social bonds, and species survival through exploration and experiencing energies. We have a dominant instinct that we feel most comfortable with and a secondary instinct to support the dominant one. The third instinct is usually the least developed, therefore, an area that manifests as an unseen personal challenge.

LEVELS OF DEVELOPMENT

The Levels of Development established by Don Riso and Russ Hudson demonstrate the varying degrees of how each type can show up in the world based on presence. Healthy, average, and unhealthy refer to the Levels of Development and the overall state of a person's ability to function. The energy of each type can show up very differently depending on how healthy or unhealthy the individual is; this is a common reason why many people mistype or feel uncomfortable as their dominant type.

Healthy—Becoming expansive and unconstricted in essence, fully present in the world

Average—Beginning to allow our egos to guide our behaviors, dropping into destructive patterns when we fall asleep to our true selves, with a fluctuation of presence

Unhealthy—Dysfunctional and destructive behaviors when ego becomes the driving force behind everything we do; falling into ego-based patterns that trap us in personality

HEALTHY	L1	BEING	Freedom from Ego Structure
	L2	ALLOWING	Psychological Capacity ("I Am")
	L3	DOING	Social Value / Gift
AVERAGE	L4	EFFORTING	Social Role / Imbalance
	L5	IMPOSING	Interpersonal Control
	L6	AGGRESSION	Overcompensation
UNHEALTHY	L7	VIOLATING	Violation
	L8	COMPULSIVE	Delusion & Compulsion
	L9	DESTROYING	Pathological Destruction

ADAPTED FROM THE RISO-HUDSON LEVELS OF DEVELOPMENT

THINGS TO REMEMBER

- There are nine points on the Enneagram map. We can access all the points but lead with one dominant type. The numbers are not a scale, meaning no type is better or worse than any other type. However, in order to keep the Enneagram energies grouped by the centers of intelligence, we look at the types in this order: Eight, Nine, One, Two, Three, Four, Five, Six, Seven.

- Your dominant Enneagram type does not change throughout your life or shift based on your home or work life. You are born into your type and your experiences adjust how you navigate life, access your wing energy, travel with the arrows, and drop into the Levels of Development.

- No type is inherently gendered or dependent on dimensions of diversity (perceived race, socioeconomic status, education, age, religion, etc.). While the descriptions and energies of the types are universal and are not dependent on certain identifying factors, it is essential to note how an Enneagram energy can vary based on cultural or environmental influences or psychological well-being. For instance, some cultures have specific gender roles, socially acceptable values, or religious influences that can impact the Enneagram energy. Still, these factors do not fundamentally change a person's dominant Enneagram type.

- No one can tell you where you stand on the Enneagram map. You find your place by reading about and exploring all aspects of the nine types. Tests can help you narrow down the choices, and you may find your type by process of elimination. Tests are not always the defining factor of where you stand on the Enneagram map; the tests' quality matters.

KEY DESCRIPTORS OF THE NINE TYPES

The descriptors for each Enneagram type listed below begin on the high side of the energy and transition into the low side of the energy.

THE BODY CENTER

8 self-confident, authoritative, hardworking, strong-willed, forceful, passionate, outspoken, independent, protective, abundant energy, maintaining power and control, defensive, combative, "invulnerable," harsh, rageful, vengeful, boastful, demonstrative, tyrannical, omnipotent

9 receptive, reassuring, agreeable, considerate, quiet, easygoing, thoughtful, accepting, supportive, accommodating, dependable, stable, hardworking, pragmatic, complacent, disengaged, emotionally indolent, indifferent, angry, stubborn, dissociated, numb, apathetic

1 principled, purposeful, organized, ethical, fastidious, fair, objective, sense of mission, practical action, high standards, inner critic, highly critical, impatient, repressed, angry, controlling, perfectionistic, puritanical, resentful, emotionally constricted, scolding, abrasive, punitive, inflexible

THE HEART CENTER

2 generous, empathetic, helpful, thoughtful, caring, reliable, compassionate, kind, overly considerate, people-pleasing, seductive, intrusive, possessive, seeking validation, angry, resentful, hurt, manipulative, flattering, demonstrative, low self-esteem/value

3 hardworking, dedicated, driven, ambitious, resourceful, impressive, motivated, highly skilled, distinguished, pragmatic, opportunistic, calculating, narcissistic, impostor syndrome, seeking validation and attention, social climber, arrogant, unprincipled, self-centered, conceited

4 emotional, empathetic, creative, unique, connected, deep, romantic, authentic, eccentric, poetic, introspective, sensitive, moody, manipulative, judgmental, self-conscious, tormented, dark, depressive, angry, lost, self-destructive, hopeless, despair, macabre, self-absorbed

THE HEAD CENTER

5 competent, capable, cerebral, wise, highly skilled, well-rounded, eccentric, pioneering, complex, perceptive, independent, inventive, visionary, secretive, withdrawn, antagonistic, cynical, argumentative, reclusive, intellectually arrogant, self-destructive, nihilistic, erratic

6 innovative, structured, hardworking, intensely loyal, reliable, security-oriented, troubleshooting, revolutionary, engaging, contradictory, dependent, indecisive, untrusting, defensive, reactive, fearful, insecure, stubborn, suspicious, erratic, worst-case scenario, panicked, paranoid

7 free-spirited, fun, happy, curious, joyful, optimistic, adventurous, fast learners, well-rounded, humorous, bold, vivacious, life of the party, flaky, self-centered, narcissistic, emotionally stunted, insensitive, impulsive, escapist mentality, erratic, compulsive, panic-stricken, avoidance, jaded

**Which descriptors from your Enneagram energy
do you resonate with the most and why?**

_____

_____

_____

_____

_____

_____

_____

_____

_____

_____

_____

_____

Enneagram Type Eight

DESCRIPTORS FOR EIGHT ENERGY

strong, assertive, self-confident, protective,
compassionate, leadership skills, heroic, determined,
driven, independent, guarded, resourceful, tough,
decisive, intimidating, confrontational, domineering,
"invulnerable," harsh, cold, vindictive, rageful,
aggressive, overbearing, bullying tendencies,
emotionally hardened, vengeful, mean-spirited

Basic Desire: to protect the self with an appearance of strength and control

Basic Fear: to be harmed or controlled by others, to be vulnerable

Core Motivation: to maintain control and strength so as to not be vulnerable and risk being harmed by others, to demonstrate self-reliance, strength, and rejection of weakness, to dominate and resist being affected by the environment, and to stay in control of all situations

Passion/The Personal Challenge: Lust—a relentless search for a challenge, cause, or recipient of/for the intensity of an overabundance of energy

Fixation/The Trap: Vengeance—a way of seeking out outlets for the angry energy, leading to the feeling that others must pay for betrayal or wrongdoing

Virtue/The Gift: Innocence—a return to a pure heart by finding strength in vulnerability and power with rather than power over others, surrendering the egoic agenda opens the heart to relinquish control and feel fully alive and free

Wings: Seven and Nine

Arrows: Two and Five

Eights want to be:

- self-reliant and in control
- able to prove strength and independence
- impactful on the environment
- assured of the unquestioned loyalty of your inner circle
- in control of any given situation
- important within inner circle
- able to stand up for self and others

Eights do not want to be:

- weak or vulnerable
- out of control
- dependent on others
- in a position to have authority questioned
- betrayed or double-crossed by trusted acquaintances or loved ones
- forced to relinquish control to someone else

LEVELS OF DEVELOPMENT
AS A TYPE EIGHT

HEALTHY LEVELS OF DEVELOPMENT

When operating within the healthy Levels of Development as an Eight, you find strength through vulnerability and a return to the purity of an innocent heart. You can take action with compassion and empathy, leading others by example into a healing space. You can become a defender from this place as you take a stand in safeguarding humanity. The emergence of your true spirit allows you to overcome the basic fear of being controlled or harmed by outside influences. You can surrender to the reality that you cannot control everything, and you harness your authentic strength as a selfless guardian and protector. As a healthy Eight, you can become one of the leaders who genuinely access their heart space and begin to operate from love and proper awareness in the face of divisiveness, confrontation, and conflict instead of attempting to confront the challenges with forged aggression. The surprising capacity for gentleness and love residing in the Eight energy is more potent than anyone expects.

AVERAGE LEVELS OF DEVELOPMENT

Most humans reside within these average levels and fluctuate up or down depending on the circumstances they find themselves in. As you drop down into the average Levels of Development, the ego agenda begins to take over. The fluctuations can create opportunities for you to pause and cultivate the presence you need to examine your thoughts and actions and course correct. This allows for you to move back up in the levels and avoid falling back into unhealthy patterns of behavior and thought. However, the fear of opening up and communicating with someone who may challenge your strength can bury your ability to find deep compassion in your big heart. As an Eight, you can express as wide a range of emotions at this level as you are willing to engage, but a wave of underlying anger usually fuels your behaviors. You can become confrontational and egocentric—benevolent one moment and belligerent the next. A mixed bag of emotions and behaviors emerges: vindictive, protective, boastful, guarded, loyal, willful, insecure, and emotionally demonstrative. This broad range of expression can be intimidating. You may share a common characteristic with other Eights at this level who feel uncertain about their surroundings, believing you must provide for and protect yourself. You build walls to keep everyone and everything out. The fear of betrayal and being let down by others can lead you to unleash a toxic energy of vengeance that alienates people and creates divides in many relationships. The opportunity to pause and engage in honest emotional reflection and objectivity becomes a struggle for Eights at this level. You may often react with forged strength and gut reactivity to conceal your vulnerability and capacity for gentleness. The anger and reactivity can morph into a wake-up call to step into a healthy space or it can deteriorate into a toxic pattern of thoughts and behaviors. It takes a great deal of self-reflection and inner work to rise up through the levels and avoid dropping further.

UNHEALTHY LEVELS OF DEVELOPMENT

When you drop into the unhealthy Levels of Development, you can become incredibly ruthless, unrelentingly cruel, vengeful, omnipotent, and highly destructive as you begin to justify your actions and beliefs from the unhealthy energy of Eight. Fear, anger, and control are the primary motivators that distort your reality, resulting in disdain for humans who may be perceived as a threat to your way of life. You become demonstrative in your cruelty and aggressively defend your beliefs to appear strong and in control. Deep down, what is being protected is your vulnerability and personal trauma. The fear of being in a weaker position can trigger a deep rage aimed at whoever or whatever is challenging your position of power. You may often find it difficult to address your internal wounds and trauma; fearing vulnerability, you will strike out and perpetually exert your energy with rage and a thirst for revenge.

You can refer back to the Levels of Development to see where you are at any point in time. Make notes on your progress below:

_____

_____

_____

_____

_____

_____

WINGS

Remember, you have access to both wings. Some people identify strongly with one wing energy over the other, but both wings still affect how your dominant type appears.

EIGHT WITH A STRONG SEVEN WING

Logical and fair decision-making, innovative and optimistic, inspirational leadership and connection, insensitive, callous, disregard for the feelings of others, difficulty listening to others

EIGHT WITH A STRONG NINE WING

Energetic and confident, protective and caring of others, supportive, able to see different perspectives, inability to control anger, stubborn and rigid, emotionally detached and overly confident, disregard for rules

ARROWS

Remember, you have access to both arrows, and you can move freely between these connections. This movement allows you to pick up positive and negative energies as needed and creates a warning system and a path for growth.

EIGHT'S ARROW TO TWO

Vulnerability seen as a strength, compassionate, caring, more open to connection, softer approach to conflict, easily offended, unrealistic expectations, emotionally demonstrative, belligerent and dismissive

EIGHT'S ARROW TO FIVE

More emotionally controlled, anger becomes a wake-up call, cautious and self-reflective, gut reactivity is slowed, isolated and withdrawn, detached from others and lacking in compassion—easily angered and provoked

INSTINCTS

As balanced human beings, we naturally have all three instincts within us. However, we have a dominant instinct that we feel most comfortable with and a secondary instinct to support the dominant one. The third instinct is usually the least developed, therefore, an area that manifests as an unseen personal challenge.

SELF-PRESERVATION EIGHT

As a Self-Preservation Eight, you may be more protective of your possessions and position and usually less sensitive toward the people around you. You tend to be more practical and focused on securing your place as impactful and essential, which is how you manage your need for power and control. You set clear boundaries and work diligently to ensure your position of power is acknowledged and respected at home and work. As a Self-Preservation Eight, you are incredibly protective of your inner circle and will make sure others know who is in charge when challenges arise.

SOCIAL EIGHT

If you are a Social Eight, you tend to focus your energy on the bonds you create with others, often cultivating a circle of trusted friends you like to test from time to time, much like the energy of a strong-willed Two. Loyalty and trust are how you exert your power and control. You enjoy a good debate, but when you feel betrayed, you will drop anyone who you think is involved in this betrayal. You can hold grudges easily and will wield your control over your social groups to make sure your position is respected. As a Social Eight, you can be more aggressive in exerting your energy outward.

SEXUAL EIGHT

If you are a Sexual Eight, your energy is focused much like the Sevens in that you are usually spontaneous and can become easily bored with anyone who cannot meet your level of intensity. You enjoy a good time and can debate and argue with humor and lightheartedness. You lean toward finding partners and an inner circle that you can reshape and form into what you want. The powerful energy of a Sexual Eight is front and center at all times. This energy can make some people uncomfortable if you are unaware of how your presence affects the people around you. It is a challenge, especially if you are unwilling to adjust how you approach the person or situation.

EIGHT'S RESPONSES TO CONFLICTS

Unhealthy Reaction

An abundance of energy and rage expressed outwardly, taking an uncompromising stance, intimidation, unwavering aggression, forceful anger, insensitivity, steamrolling of others, fear of being called out causes irrational outbursts and unreasonable language choices, resistance toward anything forced/imposed upon you, inability to access compassion, domineering stance intended to intimidate others into backing down, constantly looking for a challenge or conflict to channel whatever anger you are holding on to

Healthy Reaction

Pausing for reflection and slowing down gut reactivity, objective reasoning, finding compassion, a strong drive to protect the weak/vulnerable/mistreated/misunderstood, using your powerful stance, voice, and presence for those in need, staying a person of your word you stand up for what you believe in at all costs but with a compassionate and innocent approach, natural-born leadership tendencies, unwavering courage, truth, and determination, authentic vulnerability in showing your softer side during conflict

Reflections on your experience of unhealthy and healthy responses:

_____

_____

_____

_____

_____

_____

_____

_____

EXAMPLES OF EIGHT ENERGY

Martin Luther King Jr., Kamala Harris, Toni Morrison, Alexandria Ocasio-Cortez, Winston Churchill, Indira Gandhi, Donald Trump, Fidel Castro, G.I. Gurdjieff, Richard Wagner, Franklin D. Roosevelt, Lyndon Johnson, Mikhail Gorbachev, Golda Meir, John McCain, Pablo Picasso, Ernest Hemingway, John Wayne, Frank Sinatra

Explore your connection to one or more of these people who demonstrate strong Eight energy. What is it about their character or personality that reminds you most of yourself?

_____

_____

_____

_____

_____

_____

_____

_____

_____

_____

_____

_____

_____

_____

_____

_____

How do you experience the different elements of Eight energy within yourself?

What is your experience like with other
people who exhibit Eight energy?

_____

_____

_____

_____

_____

_____

_____

_____

_____

_____

_____

_____

_____

_____

_____

_____

_____

_____

_____

_____

_____

Reflections on

BEING AN ENNEAGRAM EIGHT

As you embark on this profound inner journey, it's essential to take a moment to revisit the very origin of your path. Within this section, we invite you to reflect upon the beginnings of your Enneagram journey and how it gently unfolded before you. Delving into past feelings and behaviors is a natural and important aspect of this process.

As an Eight, your remarkable strengths lie in your loving heart. The prompts provided here offer you a special opportunity for profound introspection.

It's quite likely that you had specific reactions when you first discovered your dominant energy as a Type Eight. These reactions are all part of the ongoing journey as you transition from mere reactions to intentional responses. It's essential to explore your feelings but not to become ensnared or overwhelmed by what you feel. Remember, feelings are transient by nature. As you navigate through your emotions, you'll discover immense fulfillment at the deeper layers of this exploration. Embrace your innate curiosity and approach this journey with the wonder of a beginner's mind as you unveil more and more about your authentic self and how you present yourself to the world. In connecting with the reality of your inner guidance and greatness, you may be pleasantly surprised by the fears that once held you back.

It's important to note that not every attribute, characteristic, or behavior described at Type Eight will necessarily resonate with your unique energy experience. This is an incredible opportunity to unearth aspects of your being that have, until now, remained hidden from your conscious awareness. This profound self-discovery journey will open your mind, mend your heart, and rejuvenate your body in ways you may have never imagined. As you dive deep into this exploration, your spirit will gracefully embrace and embody your core values, aligning with your precious gift of strength through an innocent heart. We wholeheartedly encourage you not to hold back, but to embrace this journey as it carries you to uncharted territories within your own being, revealing facets of yourself you have yet to explore. This is our heartfelt wish for you.

Grounding Meditation

As I move into self-reflection and internal exploration,
I will meditate on these prompts and gently notice
what comes up as I breathe into stillness.

I am ready to begin with three cleansing breaths.

I am releasing any tension that I am holding
in my body with each exhale.

I am grounded and present to the sensations in my body.

I am open and aware of the feelings in my heart.

I am not attached to the thoughts that float by.

I am ready to explore what being an Eight means to me.

I will embrace all aspects of my personality and gently
work toward becoming more accepting of myself.

My reactions when I discovered my dominant energy as a Type Eight:

_____

_____

_____

_____

_____

_____

_____

_____

_____

_____

_____

_____

_____

_____

_____

_____

_____

_____

_____

_____

_____

_____

My feelings about being an Eight:

_____
_____
_____
_____
_____
_____
_____
_____
_____
_____
_____
_____
_____
_____
_____
_____
_____
_____
_____
_____
_____
_____
_____
_____
_____

My hopes for discovering more about my Eight energy:

_____

_____

_____

_____

_____

_____

_____

_____

_____

_____

_____

_____

_____

_____

_____

_____

_____

_____

_____

_____

_____

My fears around seeing myself as I truly am:

_____
_____
_____
_____
_____
_____
_____
_____
_____
_____
_____
_____
_____
_____
_____
_____
_____
_____
_____
_____
_____
_____
_____
_____

Observations about myself that support Eight as my dominant type:

_____

_____

_____

_____

_____

_____

_____

_____

_____

_____

_____

_____

_____

_____

_____

_____

_____

_____

_____

_____

_____

_____

Aspects and descriptors of Eight energy that I do not feel connected with:

_____

_____

_____

_____

_____

_____

_____

_____

_____

_____

_____

Are these aspects I do not feel connected with indicators
of any personal challenges that I may overlook?

_____

_____

_____

_____

_____

_____

_____

_____

What are my core values that align with my Eight energy?

_____

_____

_____

_____

_____

_____

_____

_____

_____

_____

_____

_____

_____

_____

_____

_____

_____

_____

_____

_____

_____

_____

Reflections on my actions and beliefs around my core values:

Ways I have honored my core values recently:

_____

_____

_____

_____

_____

_____

_____

_____

_____

_____

_____

_____

_____

_____

_____

_____

_____

_____

_____

_____

What do I wish people knew about me?

Reflections on

MY EARLY MESSAGES AND EXPERIENCES

As you embark on this journey, take a moment to reflect on the early messages and messengers that have shaped your path. You might discover that your childhood experiences with the powerful energy of Type Eight instilled in you a strong internal drive to protect yourself and avoid feelings of vulnerability.

These initial reactions and responses, etched deep within you, were not merely fleeting notions but lasting imprints. You absorbed messages you may not have been consciously aware of, and they didn't simply pass through; instead, they were deeply ingrained in your very being. Retrieving them intentionally requires the assistance of a profound inner exploration.

As you transitioned into adulthood, these feelings became an integral part of your approach to life. You may have developed an internal narrative that encouraged you to channel your energy outward while preserving the delicate facets of your true self. This approach served as a shield, guarding you from external influences, and allowed you to build a protective cocoon around your warm and compassionate heart. In retrospect, this journey may reveal moments and connections deeply resonating with the energy of Type Eight.

As you reflect on your life's unfolding, who or what stands out as a pivotal influence in your development? Comparing and contrasting your life experiences, the individuals who left lasting imprints, and the indelible impressions etched in your heart is an integral part of this introspective expedition.

Being an Enneagram Eight, it's essential to resist dwelling on the negative and instead embrace the positive influences that have contributed to your strength and courage. Navigating from the assertive energy of Type Eight toward the more contemplative, rational, and gentler energies within the Enneagram may present challenges, but it also opens a direct pathway to rediscovering joy, fostering objectivity, and nurturing love. This deeper dive into your past, exploring the ups and downs of your childhood, is an opportunity to rekindle the joys that once enriched your life as a child.

Take time to unearth the childhood memories that ignited joy within you. In doing so, you'll uncover a direct route to embrace the joys of this current chapter in your life. Delve into your past to discover how these memories can transform your perception of vulnerability. Explore the contrast between taking assertive action and taking compassionate action, always remembering that you are a perpetual work in progress.

Grounding Meditation

As I move into self-reflection and internal exploration,
I will meditate on these prompts and gently notice
what comes up as I breathe into stillness.

I am ready to begin with three cleansing breaths.

I am inhaling peace and exhaling tension.

I am ready to embark on a journey into my past.

I will honor my experience as I recall childhood memories.

My past does not define me.

I can explore what was, accept what is, and embrace what will be.

My most vivid memory of how my Eight energy
showed up when I was a child:

_____

_____

_____

_____

_____

_____

_____

_____

_____

_____

_____

_____

_____

_____

_____

_____

_____

_____

_____

_____

People and experiences that have brought me
the most joy and meaning in life:

_____

_____

_____

_____

_____

_____

_____

_____

_____

_____

_____

_____

_____

_____

_____

_____

_____

_____

_____

_____

_____

_____

_____

I can create space in my life for more of these positive influences by:

_____

_____

_____

_____

_____

_____

_____

_____

_____

_____

_____

_____

_____

_____

_____

_____

_____

_____

_____

_____

_____

_____

What hopes and dreams for my future did I have as a child?

_____

_____

_____

_____

_____

_____

_____

_____

_____

_____

_____

_____

_____

_____

_____

_____

_____

_____

_____

_____

_____

Activities I enjoyed as a child:

_____

_____

_____

_____

_____

_____

_____

_____

_____

_____

_____

_____

_____

_____

_____

_____

_____

_____

_____

_____

_____

Reflections on how these activities brought
feelings of pure joy and happiness:

_____

_____

_____

_____

_____

_____

_____

_____

_____

_____

_____

_____

_____

_____

_____

_____

_____

_____

_____

_____

_____

_____

Happiness is part
of the flow of life.

If you remain rigid,
then happiness will
flow right past you.

Allow yourself
the gift of letting
go and ease into the
flow of whatever may
come your way.

I can cultivate small moments of happiness in my everyday life by:

_____

_____

_____

_____

_____

_____

_____

_____

_____

_____

_____

_____

_____

_____

_____

_____

_____

_____

_____

_____

_____

_____

Reflections on
MY PURPOSE AND
MY "PUZZLE PIECE"

Let's imagine the world as a puzzle, and envision each one of us holding a piece that, when placed, helps create a more complete and harmonious world. You possess a truly unique gift to offer to the world; imagine it as if you are the holder of a vital piece of a grand, intricate puzzle. Yet to truly offer this gift, we must be willing to embark on our own inner journey.

When we embrace this inner work, we gain the strength and clarity needed to step forward and make our unique contribution. This courageous act sets a beautiful chain reaction in motion, allowing others to find the inspiration and courage to contribute as well.

In the upcoming section, we extend a warm invitation to you, encouraging you to (re)awaken the passions and interests that stir deep within your soul, those beautiful aspects of yourself that you'd love to revive and share with the world. You might notice a strong emotional response to social injustices; this very reaction could be a hidden passion or a point of personal growth waiting to be unveiled. Your dedication to a particular societal issue could hold the key to discovering your unique place and voice in contributing to the collective healing of humanity. Perhaps your heart resonates deeply with environmental causes, or you're deeply affected by the suffering of animals. This is your precious opportunity to unearth and delve into what truly matters to you.

Consider what consistently draws your attention and captivates your mind—whether it's art, music, literature, social causes, theater, science, spirituality, parenting, or family. Why do these topics continue to surface for you? Use this opportunity to delve deeper into the aspects of your life where you find an abundance of energy or even areas that may initially appear exhausting. This is your chance to sculpt and refine your unique puzzle piece (and yes, we all have one or more) so that you can stand with gratitude and presence, fully aware of the significance of your contribution. As we awaken to our own purpose, we naturally have the capacity to awaken those around us, igniting a chain reaction of positive change.

Explore the boundless possibilities that lie ahead, and remember that your piece of the puzzle is invaluable to creating a world that's more complete, compassionate, and connected.

Grounding Meditation

As I move into self-reflection and internal exploration,
I will meditate on these prompts and gently notice
what comes up as I breathe into stillness.

I am ready to begin with three cleansing breaths.

I am releasing any tension that I am holding
in my body with each exhale.

I am inhaling into the wholeness of the Universe
and exhaling whatever may be troubling me.

I am open to exploring my place in the world.

I am willing to explore my purpose and (re)discover the
unique puzzle piece I hold to contribute to the world.

My life has meaning, and my presence matters.

I am accepting of whatever comes up for me at this moment.

What contributions do I want to make in this world?

Reflections on how I align my daily actions with my
deeper sense of strength and control:

_____

_____

_____

_____

_____

_____

_____

_____

_____

_____

_____

_____

_____

_____

_____

_____

_____

_____

_____

_____

_____

_____

_____

_____

_____

What inspires me?

_____

_____

_____

_____

_____

_____

_____

_____

_____

_____

_____

_____

_____

_____

_____

_____

_____

_____

_____

_____

_____

_____

_____

_____

How have I limited myself in finding sources of inspiration? How can I open myself to new experiences? Have I considered engaging with new people, places, music, art, literature, and so on?

What comes up for me when I think about the activities, relationships, and causes that I am drawn to?

_____

_____

_____

_____

_____

_____

_____

_____

_____

_____

_____

_____

_____

_____

_____

_____

_____

_____

_____

_____

_____

_____

I am very passionate about:

_____

_____

_____

_____

_____

_____

_____

_____

_____

_____

_____

_____

_____

_____

_____

_____

_____

_____

_____

_____

_____

_____

_____

The quality
of your life
will reflect
how deep you
are willing
to go to touch
your own soul.

What personal, professional, spiritual, and/or life
roles contribute to my sense of identity?

_____

_____

_____

_____

_____

_____

_____

_____

_____

_____

_____

_____

_____

_____

_____

_____

_____

_____

_____

_____

_____

What leadership roles do I find myself drawn to
in my life and what does that look like?

_____

_____

_____

_____

_____

_____

_____

_____

_____

_____

_____

_____

_____

_____

_____

_____

_____

_____

_____

_____

_____

What am I willing to do for others to make the world a better place?

Reflections on my current projects, work, and/or endeavors:

How are these feeding my spirit or draining my energy?

Reflections on

HOW MY EIGHT
ENERGY SHOWS UP

As an individual standing firm at Type Eight on the Enneagram, your journey is marked by a compelling aversion to vulnerability and a strong inclination to maintain control over the people and circumstances in your life. These tendencies deeply influence the way your energy manifests. When you're operating within the average Levels of Development you may find yourself feeling justified in your actions and at ease with your behaviors, all while harboring a subtle apprehension about exposing your true, vulnerable self.

For those who resonate with Type Eight, there exists a profound sense of fairness that naturally emerges. This sense of justice, trust, and strength often plays a central role in establishing the standards for any given situation. However, when you deviate from your true heart and slip into a default state of wielding power over others instead of empowering them, your pursuit of raising your energy's vibration to a healthier level can become distorted, morphing into a quest for vengeance.

This is where the transformative process of inner work becomes paramount. The journey entails realigning your inner anger with the principles of justice, peace, and compassion. Releasing the hold of anger and letting go of the thirst for vengeance opens the path to alignment with spirit. In this space, love, loyalty, and a genuine ability to trust humanity as a whole supplant wrath and harsh actions. You become receptive to a more gentle and kind approach, ultimately embracing the flow of life as a precious gift.

In this openhearted state of presence, you radiate an aura that attracts and resonates with others. Your impact on the world around you is not only acknowledged but warmly welcomed. You become the embodiment of love, and your capacity for gentleness and compassion enriches your interactions, bringing about a sense of deep connection and harmony. By embracing this transformative journey, you can step into a brighter, more inviting space where your influence is truly valued and celebrated.

Grounding Meditation

As I move into self-reflection and internal exploration,
I will meditate on these prompts and gently notice
what comes up as I breathe into stillness.

I am ready to begin with three cleansing breaths.

I am releasing any tension that I am holding
in my body with each exhale.

I am inhaling into presence and exhaling negativity and judgment.

I am ready to explore my Eightness.

I will allow myself to reflect on how I show up to myself and others.

I will acknowledge any feelings that arise with
Grace and compassion for myself.

I will embrace all parts of my being as valid and valuable.

I will release the fear of being vulnerable and allow myself the
compassion and space I need to process whatever surfaces.

Reflect back on the "Levels of Development" section (page 14) for this exercise.

I was aware of the high side of my Eight energy this week when:

_____

_____

_____

_____

_____

_____

_____

_____

_____

_____

_____

_____

_____

_____

_____

_____

_____

_____

_____

_____

Reflect back on the "Levels of Development" section (page 14) for this exercise.

I was aware of the low side of my Eight energy this week when:

_____

_____

_____

_____

_____

_____

_____

_____

_____

_____

_____

_____

_____

_____

_____

_____

_____

_____

_____

_____

_____

It is in our most vulnerable moments that great opportunities for personal and emotional growth are manifested.

My reflections on vulnerability and what it means to me:

_____

_____

_____

_____

_____

_____

_____

_____

_____

_____

_____

_____

_____

_____

_____

_____

_____

_____

_____

_____

_____

_____

_____

_____

My reactions to feeling betrayed:

_____
_____
_____
_____
_____
_____
_____
_____
_____
_____
_____
_____
_____
_____
_____
_____
_____
_____
_____
_____
_____
_____
_____
_____

When do I feel that others perceive me as being "too much"?

_____

_____

_____

_____

_____

_____

_____

_____

_____

_____

_____

_____

_____

_____

_____

_____

_____

_____

_____

_____

_____

_____

_____

_____

How do I express love and affection?

What parts of myself do I hide from others and why?

_____
_____
_____
_____
_____
_____
_____
_____
_____
_____
_____
_____
_____
_____
_____
_____
_____
_____
_____
_____
_____
_____
_____
_____
_____

What do other people do for me that makes me feel seen?

How do I make others feel seen?

_____
_____
_____
_____
_____
_____
_____
_____
_____
_____
_____
_____
_____
_____
_____
_____
_____
_____
_____
_____
_____
_____
_____

You must embrace
your own being
and accept yourself
exactly as you are.
This is a first
step in belonging.
Never let anyone
determine whether
or not you belong.

That choice is yours.

What does belonging mean to me? How have I sought
out belonging and connection in my life?

_____

_____

_____

_____

_____

_____

_____

_____

_____

_____

_____

_____

_____

_____

_____

_____

_____

_____

_____

_____

_____

How do other people describe me?

Fill the page with words, phrases, and drawings.
Allow for the flow of creativity and freedom.

How do I describe myself?

Fill the page with words, phrases, and drawings.
Allow for the flow of creativity and freedom.

Reflections on

POWER, CONTROL, AND VULNERABILITY

In your inner work journey as an Eight, it's important to recognize that power and control often play a significant role in how you navigate the world. You possess an inherent drive to maintain control over your life and your environment, and this determination radiates from you, touching the lives of those around you.

The potent energy that resides within you, as well as the manner in which you harness it to acquire or uphold control and power, varies from person to person and is deeply rooted in your unique perspective. Regardless of what control and power look like for you as an Eight, the underlying motivations often revolve around safeguarding yourself from external influences. For some, it's a means to shield against feelings of vulnerability or perceived weakness, while for others, it serves as a protective boundary against potential physical and psychological harm. Your Eight energy is marked by actively asserting your autonomy and resisting external influences in all aspects of your life.

As an Eight, it's likely that early life experiences have left indelible marks, shaping your instinct to avoid vulnerability, weakness, or being under someone's control. To safeguard your innocence, you've constructed a protective barrier around your heart, perhaps influenced by direct or indirect messages that revealing your vulnerability could lead to you being hurt or controlled by others. It's important to recognize that these narratives, though deeply ingrained, can be unraveled through intentional and profound inner work.

During this transformative process, remember to be gentle and compassionate with yourself. As you begin to reclaim your vulnerability, you'll come to realize that the walls you've erected, while meant to shield you from pain, have also inadvertently kept love at bay. Your true heart doesn't require defense, and as you embrace the tenderness within, you'll witness those walls gradually crumble, creating a more welcoming space for the warmth and richness of love and light to flow into your life.

Grounding Meditation

As I move into self-reflection and internal exploration,
I will meditate on these prompts and gently notice
what comes up as I breathe into stillness.

I am ready to begin with three cleansing breaths.

I am inhaling peace and love and exhaling judgment and criticism.

I acknowledge that I have an aversion to vulnerability
and I am willing to explore what is underneath.

I can accept that power with is different from power over.

I can examine my need to maintain control and my
need to create boundaries all while working to be
more open-minded, receptive, and reflective.

I will access Grace and loving-kindness as I honor
the function of my inner narrative.

I will remain in presence and choose a path
of empathy and compassion.

What boundaries do I create, and what are they protecting me from?

What does betrayal look like for me, and how does it feel?

_____
_____
_____
_____
_____
_____
_____
_____
_____
_____
_____
_____
_____
_____
_____
_____
_____
_____
_____
_____
_____
_____
_____
_____
_____

What are my reactions when I begin to feel
powerless, out of control, or vulnerable?

_____

_____

_____

_____

_____

_____

_____

_____

_____

_____

_____

_____

_____

_____

_____

_____

_____

_____

_____

_____

How does this affect how I treat others?

_____
_____
_____
_____
_____
_____
_____
_____
_____
_____
_____
_____
_____
_____
_____
_____
_____
_____
_____
_____
_____
_____

What am I willing to let go of in order to allow
people to see my vulnerability?

_____

_____

_____

_____

_____

_____

_____

_____

_____

_____

_____

_____

_____

_____

_____

_____

_____

_____

_____

_____

_____

Who do I allow to see my vulnerable side and why?

Can I consider an opposing view on something I care deeply about, and what would that look like? How can I explore this further?

What does it look like when I release control to
someone else and everything is okay?

What steps can I take to pause and change my course of action
when I notice my need to control things has taken over?

Reflecting back on how I may have been overly reactive or harsh,
how could I have handled certain situations differently?

We are surrounded by Grace in every moment of our lives. Grace always comes through when we allow ourselves to embrace and experience the warmth of its existence. Let love and light in.

Allow Grace to lead your actions today.

What does Grace look like for me as a Eight?

Reflections on

MY RELATIONSHIP TO ANGER

As an Eight, you might find yourself facing a formidable wall of anger and rage surrounding an unhealed or unexplored internal wound. This metaphorical wall can act as a barrier, concealing your authentic self, and how you choose to address or confront it is a deeply personal journey. This internal turmoil often stems from early memories of betrayal, rejection, neglect, feeling unimportant, or struggling with feelings of inadequacy. Each person approaches this barrier uniquely, and when we find ourselves ensnared in a toxic behavioral pattern, this internal anger can often manifest as outward expressions directed at others.

In your efforts to protect yourself, you've built formidable walls, making it a challenge for others to get close to you. The fear of betrayal and the potential for disappointment can lead to the release of a toxic energy of vengeance, which can strain relationships and create divisions. Engaging in honest self-reflection and embracing emotional objectivity can be an uphill battle at times. You may often react with a facade of strength and gut reactions, all in a bid to shield your vulnerability and capacity for gentleness. This is where the journey of inner work comes into play.

Anger and forgiveness, intertwined companions in the human experience, form a complex concept often misunderstood. Beyond benefiting others, forgiveness frees you from emotional burdens, opening the path to love and happiness. It enables your authentic expression of love, aligning with your creation. Great ascended masters stress the importance of forgiveness, providing invaluable lessons we sometimes forget. Remember, forgiveness is integral to self-love, allowing your authentic self to return to innocence and purity by freeing yourself from pain. It's the ultimate act of self-respect, empowering and embracing your inner strength.

In this section, you'll have the opportunity to reflect and explore your anger, taking the first steps toward addressing it in a constructive manner. Be patient and compassionate with yourself as you delve deeper into this exploration. These exercises are thoughtfully designed to guide you through the challenges of your energy, allowing you to reconnect with the inherent goodness, love, and light that reside within you. Embrace this journey with an open heart and a spirit of self-compassion, for it is a step toward unleashing the richness of your authentic self.

Grounding Meditation

As I move into self-reflection and internal exploration,
I will meditate on these prompts and gently notice
what comes up as I breathe into stillness.

I am ready to begin with three cleansing breaths.

I am inhaling a sense of calm and peace and
exhaling tension, anxiety, and anger.

I acknowledge my anger and am willing to
gently explore what's underneath.

I will explore my relationship to my anger
with patience and understanding.

I accept anger as a natural human emotion.

My anger does not define who I am.

I will accept my anger as an internal warning system to
seek out opportunities for growth and self-reflection.

What/who makes me angry?

_____
_____
_____
_____
_____
_____
_____
_____
_____
_____
_____
_____
_____
_____
_____
_____
_____
_____
_____
_____
_____
_____
_____
_____

How do I express my anger? What does it look like?

When does my anger turn into rage and vengeance,
and what does that look like?

_____

_____

_____

_____

_____

_____

_____

_____

_____

_____

_____

_____

_____

_____

_____

_____

_____

_____

_____

_____

What does it look like when my anger becomes a
barrier between me and those I care about?

_____

_____

_____

_____

_____

_____

_____

_____

_____

_____

_____

_____

_____

_____

_____

_____

_____

_____

_____

What are my reactions to feeling betrayed or
let down by those closest to me?

_____

_____

_____

_____

_____

_____

_____

_____

_____

_____

_____

_____

_____

_____

_____

_____

_____

_____

_____

_____

_____

What do I need to do to allow myself the space to
pause before reacting or unleashing my anger?

_____

_____

_____

_____

_____

_____

_____

_____

_____

_____

_____

_____

_____

_____

_____

_____

_____

_____

_____

What am I willing to surrender to allow myself to release the anger?

_____

_____

_____

_____

_____

_____

_____

_____

_____

_____

_____

_____

_____

_____

_____

_____

_____

_____

_____

What aspects of my life allow me to soften my approach and create a space where I can be supportive and compassionate?

What/who do I need to forgive?

Forgiveness doesn't excuse their behavior.
Forgiveness prevents their behavior
from destroying your heart.
UNKNOWN

Do I know how to forgive? What is holding me back from
accessing forgiveness for myself and others?

_____

_____

_____

_____

_____

_____

_____

_____

_____

_____

_____

_____

_____

_____

_____

_____

_____

_____

_____

_____

MY VIRTUE OF INNOCENCE

As an Eight the virtue that beckons you is the gentle and inviting embrace of innocence. This concept becomes all the more attainable when you view it as a free-flowing energy, a guiding force that allows your true heart to flourish in a realm of boundless strength, compassion, and vulnerability. The precious gift of innocence empowers you to embrace life's opportunities with the fervor of love and benevolence, using your energy for the greater good. Innocence is able to flourish from within you when you've committed to the inner work and tapped into the high side of Eight energy.

Throughout your quest to embrace your virtue, you will encounter some familiar obstacles along the way. The allure of vengeance, the fixation of Type Eight, can be particularly challenging to navigate. The fear of vulnerability or ceding control to others often leads to a release of energy, an eternal push to guard and protect yourself. This is precisely where the inner work process comes to life. As you work through these inner barriers, you begin to feel secure in your ability to let your softer side emerge. You realize that you cannot control everything, and in this realization, you harness your authentic strength as a compassionate guardian and protector of the innocent heart within each one of us.

With newfound understanding, you can take action with empathy and Grace, leading by example and guiding others toward spaces of healing and benevolence. This is your invitation to step into a transformative realm, one where you rekindle your innate strength through the purity of your heart. The incredible well of gentleness and love within the Eight energy holds more power than one might expect. Here you discover your balance and connection with the world, a space where you can fully embody the virtue of innocence.

Your journey to rediscover your connection to innocence is a vital step in unveiling your authentic self. As you delve into this path, it's important to remain present and open-minded, allowing your capacity for compassion, benevolence, and strength through vulnerability to reawaken. This is the space where you truly embrace your virtue of innocence and, in doing so, bring love, connection, and compassion to all those who share in your life's journey.

Grounding Meditation

As I move into self-reflection and internal exploration,
I will meditate on each of these prompts and gently notice
what comes up for me as I breathe into stillness.

I am ready to begin with three cleansing breaths.

I am inhaling into innocence and exhaling any
hesitation or anger I may be holding on to.

As I explore innocence, I seek out opportunities
to allow it to flow naturally.

Innocence is my access to Grace.

Innocence is always present within me.

I allow myself to embrace the gift of innocence
by releasing what no longer serves me.

How has innocence manifested in my life, and what did it bring?

How has innocence eluded me?
What comes up for me by asking this question?

Innocence is the untainted essence of the heart that reveals our true nature.

What am I willing to surrender to embrace innocence?

_____
_____
_____
_____
_____
_____
_____
_____
_____
_____
_____
_____
_____
_____
_____
_____
_____
_____
_____
_____
_____
_____
_____
_____

When do I notice my tendency toward vengeance and anger fading and my ability to access the virtue of innocence developing?

_____

_____

_____

_____

_____

_____

_____

_____

_____

_____

_____

_____

_____

_____

_____

_____

_____

_____

_____

_____

_____

_____

Reflecting on my need for control, my aversion to vulnerability, and my relationship with anger, can I explore what my path to the embodiment of innocence looks like?

What challenges do I face when I am trying to access my capacity for innocence, compassion, and kindness?

_____

_____

_____

_____

_____

_____

_____

_____

_____

_____

_____

_____

_____

_____

_____

_____

_____

_____

_____

_____

_____

_____

_____

_____

What/who makes me want to be kinder and more compassionate and why?

_____

_____

_____

_____

_____

_____

_____

_____

_____

_____

_____

_____

_____

_____

_____

_____

_____

_____

_____

_____

_____

_____

_____

What does it look like when I allow people to see how gentle, caring, and warm-hearted I can be? How does it make me feel?

What are a few mantras I will use daily to bring myself back to the present
and move into a space where I can access the virtue of innocence?

Example: I will let go of the things that I cannot control
and find a way to allow my pure heart to emerge.

_____

_____

_____

_____

_____

_____

_____

_____

_____

_____

_____

_____

_____

_____

_____

_____

_____

_____

_____

_____

Discovering Connections to

OTHER ENNEAGRAM ENERGIES

Consider the Enneagram energies as nine individual gifts, each uniquely enriching the tapestry of your being. Within each of us, these nine energies coexist, and far too often, our fixation on our Enneagram type limits our perspective, hindering exploration of the eight other invaluable energies residing within us. It's vital to recognize that every human being requires the presence of these nine energies to achieve wholeness and completeness.

At each point of the Enneagram, a precious gift awaits, illuminating the path of self-discovery. At point One the gift is integrity, a beacon that guides you with a resolute moral compass. Point Two bestows the gift of pure love, fostering a spirit of generosity and an open heart for giving and receiving. Point Three endows you with the drive to accomplish and achieve great things, not just for personal gain but for the greater good of all. Point Four graces you with the capacity to embrace the world's beauty, holding it through love, empathy, and profound compassion while connecting deeply with human emotions. Point Five gifts you with the power of observation and the ability to discern solutions that might otherwise go unnoticed. At point Six you receive the gift of resilience, enabling you to cultivate the awareness of what is needed to keep us all protected, prepared, and unwavering in the face of adversity. Point Seven brings the gift of optimism, positivity, and spontaneity, infusing even the most challenging tasks with the spirit of joyfulness. Point Eight's gift is leadership, guiding us forward with the purity and strength of an innocent heart, always mindful of keeping our collective well-being intact. Finally, at point Nine, you are blessed with the gift of pure peace, a peace that transcends understanding and can only arise from a heart transformed by light and love.

Imagine that someone has lovingly gifted you with these nine beautifully wrapped presents. Why would you choose to open only one?

In this section, you are encouraged to embark on a journey through all nine Enneagram energies, to explore the connections to your wings, lines, and arrows, as well as the points that may not be part of your primary access. It's important to remember that you always have access to all nine energies, and sometimes, it takes a more deliberate effort to unearth these connections. Embrace this exploration with an open heart, for it's a step toward a deeper understanding of your authentic, multifaceted self, filled with infinite possibilities.

Grounding Meditation

As I move into self-reflection and internal exploration,
I will meditate on these prompts and gently notice
what comes up as I breathe into stillness.

I am ready to begin with three cleansing breaths.

I am inhaling into expansiveness and exhaling constriction.

I have the gift of all nine Enneagram energies within me.

I can freely explore my energy at all nine points.

I am not limited by my type.

I acknowledge my energy and connection to point Two and
point Five and utilize them for growth and awareness.

I can freely access my wings at point Seven and point Nine.

THE BODY CENTER: 8-9-1

In the Body Center, we gain access to our body's wisdom and gut intuition. The Body Center energy is focused on action—affecting the world or environment to avoid being influenced, controlled, or limited by it, and expressing anger or rage in different ways.

What does it look like for me to access
the energies within the Body Center?

Eight

_____

_____

_____

_____

_____

Nine

_____

_____

_____

_____

_____

One

_____

_____

_____

_____

_____

THE HEART CENTER: 2-3-4

In the Heart Center, we gain access to our capacity for emotional honesty and human connection. The Heart Center energy is focused on emotions, self-image, and value—determining your identity and the value you place on your identity plays a key role in how you access the Heart Center energy.

What does it look like for me to access the
energies within the Heart Center?

Two

_____

_____

_____

_____

_____

Three

_____

_____

_____

_____

_____

Four

_____

_____

_____

_____

_____

THE HEAD CENTER: 5-6-7

In the Head Center, we gain access to our ability to reflect, process, and internalize information. The wisdom we have access to in the Head Center energies allows us to cultivate the space we need for objectivity and inner guidance.

What does it look like for me to access the
energies within the Head Center?

Five

_____
_____
_____
_____
_____

Six

_____
_____
_____
_____
_____

Seven

_____
_____
_____
_____
_____

Do I face any challenges when connecting to particular
Enneagram energies? Can I explore this further?

_____

_____

_____

_____

_____

_____

_____

_____

_____

_____

_____

_____

_____

_____

_____

_____

_____

_____

_____

_____

_____

_____

Reflecting on the connection to my Seven wing, how can Seven energy help me become more optimistic, joyful, and innovative?

*The great science to live happily
is to live in the present.*

PYTHAGORAS

Reflecting on the connection to my Nine wing, how can Nine energy bring me perspective, peace, and a sense of harmony in all things?

_____

_____

_____

_____

_____

_____

_____

_____

_____

_____

_____

_____

_____

_____

_____

_____

_____

_____

_____

_____

_____

_____

Today, I choose awareness. I choose to be aware of the beauty of life and living. I choose to be aware of the simple pleasures in life. I choose awareness of joy, awareness of peace, and awareness of love.

IYANLA VANZANT

At point Eight, I share a connection to point Two, which provides an opportunity to explore the gifts and challenges of this energy. On the upside, this energy can help me deal with emotions as they arise and allow for my innocent heart to emerge in full force. On the downside, this energy can make me manipulative and emotionally demonstrative. How have I experienced Two energy in my life?

_____

_____

_____

_____

_____

_____

_____

_____

_____

_____

_____

_____

_____

_____

_____

_____

_____

_____

_____

Self-love is an ocean and your heart is a vessel.
Make it full, and any excess will spill over into the
lives of the people you hold dear.
But you must come first.

BEAU TAPLIN

What does it look like when I tap into the compassion, gentleness, generosity, and strength through vulnerability at point Two? How does my connection to point Two affect my actions, behaviors, and beliefs?

_____

_____

_____

_____

_____

_____

_____

_____

_____

_____

_____

_____

_____

_____

_____

_____

_____

_____

_____

_____

_____

Care for your psyche . . . . know thyself, for once we know ourselves, we may learn how to care for ourselves.

SOCRATES

At point Eight, I share a connection to point Five, which provides an opportunity to explore the gifts and challenges of this energy. On the upside, this energy can allow for space to reflect, find objectivity, and use my anger as a wake-up call. On the downside, this energy can make me feel detached and dampen my ability to cultivate compassion and connection. How have I experienced Five energy in my life?

Accept yourself, love yourself, and keep moving forward. If you want to fly, you have to give up what weighs you down.

ROY T. BENNETT

What does it look like when I am able to channel the focus, space for reflection, and objectivity at point Five? How does my connection to point Five affect my actions, behaviors, and beliefs?

_____

_____

_____

_____

_____

_____

_____

_____

_____

_____

_____

_____

_____

_____

_____

_____

_____

_____

_____

_____

_____

There are two ways of spreading light:
to be the candle or the mirror that reflects it.

EDITH WHARTON

Resources for

CONTINUED EXPLORATION

If you would like to continue your Enneagram journey,
we invite you to visit our resources hub at:

DEBORAHEGERTON.COM/RESOURCES

and explore all of the resources we have gathered for you.
This resource hub is updated frequently, so make sure you
check back when you feel the need for a little inspiration.

You are also encouraged to read my books:

*Know Justice Know Peace: A Transformative Journey of Social Justice,
Anti-Racism, and Healing through the Power of the Enneagram*

*Enneagram Made Easy: Explore the Nine Personality Types of the
Enneagram to Open Your Heart, Find Joy, and Discover Your True Self*

**For easy access to the resources hub, use
your smartphone to scan this QR code:**

ABOUT THE AUTHOR

Deborah Threadgill Egerton, Ph.D., is an internationally respected psychotherapist, best-selling author, certified Enneagram teacher, unity and belonging advocate for the healing of humanity, consultant, coach, and spiritual teacher. Dr. Egerton specializes in working with the Enneagram to facilitate intentional change in individuals and organizations.

Affectionately referred to as "Dr. E," she has attained IEA Certification with Distinction for her groundbreaking utilization of the Enneagram in the realm of humanitarian healing. Her work is dedicated to dismantling marginalization and transcending the divisive practice of "othering," offering a guiding path toward the harmonious unification of our global community through the transformative forces of kindness and compassion. Dr. E serves as the president of the International Enneagram Association, the global entity responsible for educating, certifying, and accrediting practitioners, teachers, and schools. In her tenure with the IEA, she has been instrumental in fostering an environment of greater inclusivity and accessibility within the global Enneagram community. Her unwavering commitment to justice, equity, diversity, and inclusion has earned her the affectionate title of "Enneagram JEDI" among her peers.

Dr. E extends her coaching and mentoring expertise to a diverse spectrum of individuals, including best-selling authors, top-tier executives, spiritual luminaries, accomplished therapists, and a myriad of coaches, each hailing from distinct and varied backgrounds. For more than two decades, her work has focused on guiding humanity toward a deeper and more compassionate approach to inner work by harnessing the insights of the Enneagram. Her innovative approach to using the Enneagram in social justice and anti-racism work created a blueprint to reconnect people across all dimensions of diversity and has been implemented in various organizations and entities across the globe. She focuses her work on individuals and organizations to help them release false historical narratives and open their minds and hearts to a more compassionate and connected approach to life.

We hope you enjoyed this Hay House book. If you'd like to receive our online catalog featuring additional information on Hay House books and products, or if you'd like to find out more about the Hay Foundation, please contact:

Hay House LLC, P.O. Box 5100, Carlsbad, CA 92018-5100
(760) 431-7695 or (800) 654-5126
www.hayhouse.com® • www.hayfoundation.org

———

Published in Australia by:
Hay House Australia Publishing Pty Ltd
18/36 Ralph St., Alexandria NSW 2015
Phone: +61 (02) 9669 4299
www.hayhouse.com.au

Published in the United Kingdom by:
Hay House UK Ltd
The Sixth Floor, Watson House,
54 Baker Street, London W1U 7BU
Phone: +44 (0) 203 927 7290
www.hayhouse.co.uk

Published in India by:
Hay House Publishers (India) Pvt Ltd
Muskaan Complex, Plot No. 3,
B-2, Vasant Kunj, New Delhi 110 070
Phone: +91 11 41761620
www.hayhouse.co.in

———

<u>Access New Knowledge.</u>
<u>Anytime. Anywhere.</u>

Learn and evolve at your own pace
with the world's leading experts.

www.hayhouseU.com